Among Women

Among Women

POEMS BY

Jason Shinder

Graywolf Press

Saint Paul, Minnesota

Publication of this volume is made possible in part by a grant provided by the Minnesota State Arts Board through an appropriation by the Minnesota State Legislature, and by a grant from the National Endowment for the Arts. Significant support has also been provided by the Bush Foundation; Dayton's Project Imagine with support from Target Foundation; the McKnight Foundation; a grant made on behalf of the Stargazer Foundation; and other generous contributions from foundations, corporations, and individuals. To these organizations and individuals we offer our heartfelt thanks.

Published by Graywolf Press
2402 University Avenue, Suite 203
Saint Paul, MN 55114

www.graywolfpress.org

Published in the United States of America

ISBN: 1-55597-320-5

2   4   6   8   9   7   5   3   1
First Graywolf Printing, 2001

Library of Congress Catalog Number: 00-107647

Cover art: Edward Hopper, *Excursion into Philosophy*, 1959
   (Private Collection)
Section title designs by Nancy Modlin Katz

Cover design: Scott Sorenson

Contents

for my brother, Martin

The body waits for love to give it meaning. We discover, finally, this love is at the center of our peril and our salvation.

—*James Baldwin*

The One Secret That Has Carried

Irene loves a man
        who is afraid of sex—
                she's attended

to everything,
        said it was okay,
                held me until I slept.

She says, *Why don't you just
        not think about it?*
                But I want to know

every sensation,
        nothing untouched,
                though I pull my hand away

once she's found it.
        I can't be around a woman
                too long,

too much.
        I say, *I was mistreated.*
                She says, *A cup of tea?*

I say, *I can't start a thing*
        and then
                describe the kind

of thing I'd start.
        We talk about ballrooms,
                long sleeves and sashes,

say someday
    we should go somewhere
        though we can't think

of anywhere
    and then I say abruptly,
        I've never loved

hard enough
    to be loved back.
        I say it as if I've had enough

of the whole goddamn
    world and will never
        be satisfied.

I'm looking
    at the wall.
        She's looking out

the window because
    she needs
        to be somewhere.

Later, I leave a note:
    Sorry for the difficulties.
        Meaning: how come

you don't leave?
    I've never told this story.
        Even at the moment

of dying,
      I would say
            it was someone else's.

Into an Occasion for Celebration

I'm afraid
  if I come
    I'll sound like someone

I don't know—
  louder, deeper,
    and repeating

every soft-flung syllable,
  salt-spray
    of irregular breathing.

Even the possibility
  of it
    doesn't move me,

thinking about it
  in front of her.
    Excited and wanting

more than life
  and longer
    to fuck her, a wave

from the deepest surf
  of the blood
    gathers itself up inside

and then
  abruptly stops.
    I'm from another planet, I say,

opening a bottle of wine
      on the bed.
            I can change, I think,

before the dark does,
      a city hushed
            reduced to breathing

into her ear
      for so long
            the moon's

no longer round
      but a tunnel
            toward the river.

A Woman's Company

My desire
        was this terrible thing
                inside of me

and I imagined nothing
        that might help it
                except another photo

of a woman's breasts
        hanging just
                above the navel.

It was good
        if she pressed
                her forefinger

between a man's lips,
        good if she was kind.
                And then maybe

her plum lips,
        her body's blond hairs
                coming into bed—

the slip of a hand
        across thousands of miles
                of nothing,

no one.
        And then opening
                my mouth

to sigh
      without being heard
           and looking about

to see if the ghosts
      of anyone I knew
           were watching.

Masturbation

I saw a woman coming near
and thought, this is the center of my life.

In the dark, in the quiet hours, I dreamed
it was a woman who belonged wherever I was.

I desired her so much I stood for hours
against the screen door of my father's house.

My Father's House

My father worked
> behind a counter
>> of meats

in a delicatessen,
> and when he was alone
>> he lay down

on his belly
> and pressed his face
>> into every pore

of a pillow.
> Even his new green
>> four-door sedan

drifting above
> the open roads
>> could not make him

feel at ease.
> He taught me
>> to work

without knowing
> I was working
>> and when he laughed

he was so close,
> so far away.
>> Cigarette in mouth,

denim shirt open,
    leather boots,
        heels with cleats —

I only appeared
    to be among women.
        I was already his.

Among Men

Even at the moment
    of kissing a girl
        because

I was a boy—
    there was always
        another boy

looking to see
    how long
        I could place

my lips
    on her lips
        without stopping

without ever knowing
    I was kissing.
        And then

what to tell the guys
    coming out
        of their coats,

asking, *How'd it go?*
    Meaning:
        did I get any?

*Why don't you
    just get laid?*
        my father said.

Getting Laid

What did I know of the way to share
a couch, half our bodies under a big blanket?

My fingers moved down the buttons
of her blouse, moved a little further down.

If I tried to lie still as if on grass,
the grass was slippery.

How far to the end of the evening?

I could not bring pleasure to myself
without thinking of betrayal. Yet she was on my hand.

Part of the Body

It's not that her blouse
      isn't opening.
            If I say anything

I'm a liar. It's just
      nobody lives here.
            Or it's late.

Or I'm tired. Maybe
      lie down lightly
            or sideways,

go back home
      before dinner.
            I can only bear

one part of the body
      at a time,
            the fear the fear and the fear.

The Fear

I waited for love
    the way my dog waited
        for someone

to call him
    by his real name.
        I ripped open

my shirt,
    wanting to be saved
        but not knowing

from what.
    After each breath,
        the next was smaller,

troubled.
    I didn't want to die,
        an orange

that has spent its life
    in the dark.
        Sometimes my speech

made no sound
    and the moon
        was a sinking ship

in its last hour.
    And sometimes
        the people I knew

I blamed them
        and the house I grew up in
            was burning.

My Mother's House

My mother sat
        by the window
                waiting

for my father
        to return.
                Cars drifted by

without drivers.
        Houselights went off,
                went on.

Sometimes
        my father was afraid
                to look

at the beauty
        in his wife's face
                as she opened

the front door—her eyes
        turned inward,
                wearing

the white T-shirt
        she'd worn
                the night before.

How are you?
        she asked.
                I don't know, he said.

Growing Up

The trouble with me
       is I don't know
             if my penis

is too small
       and I don't know
             who to ask.

Sometimes, for days,
       I don't think
             about it

but then I wake,
       T-shirt ripped
             from which it seems

the sea
       has been dripping,
             wool blanket

turned down low
       on the bed
             which has something

to do with dying.
       If only the world
             were blind.

If only
       my fingers
             would fall off.

Something can be done?
I asked Doctor Goldstein,
his left hand

round the bottom
of my balls
when I coughed.

Why don't you
save your money,
he said.

A Crowd Stands for One Person

There was an old card
    I found in an old shop
        on Sunrise Highway—

two angels
    who didn't hesitate
        to kiss each other's lips.

I walked into the market
    with the greatest of ease
        and bought a beer

and low-fat potato chips.
    And a woman strolled in
        and purchased a quart of milk

and no one admitted
    it was something else
        she wanted.

We sat around
    a fireplace and dreamed
        we had a fire burning

inside us,
    too. Sure,
        I was standing before

the window as if
    it were a natural part
        of life. I had something

I meant to say.
    It was
        a rare moment

when the loves
    of the future
        walked from the fire.

About a Man

To touch a woman was nothing
and less than nothing

was the way I touched myself.

From nothing nothing could come.
From nothing nothing could be taken.

Madness Frequently Discovers Itself

In August the salt-spray
      of the sea-town
            I live in settles

on the sidewalks.
      And the one eating
            with his mouth open,

talking endlessly about shoes,
      is gazing out
            on the harbor.

I hate him because
      to say he is mad is to say
            his troubles are not

like mine. I find others
      like me, hands in pockets,
            walking into the movie theater,

their voices softening
      with a faint melody
            as the houselights go

off-white to yellow, black—
      all of us partners
            against the bright world.

One Day I Will Love

It will be late.
    The stars
        will help me.

How I like
    to be
        the only one,

a bullfrog
    deep in the woods.
        And watching

from a distance.
    Shadows
        of friends.

What am I?
    A lovely man?
        I don't even want

to die.
    Open the window, I say,
        trapped in the glass

but then move
    as if moving
        from within.

I know
    who keeps shifting
        the wind.

Angels
      with no wings.
            I throw seeds

into the open air—
      long boughs of
            purple lilacs

as if
      this is not a world
            with too much

on it.
      No animals
            on the front steps.

What Gets in the Way of Love Is Love

Irene was on her knees,
    filling her mouth
        with my penis,

when I turned my head
    and became dizzy.
        When she lifted herself

away from my body,
    lay down on the sheets
        on the mattress,

she pushed a pillow over the bed
    with one hand.
        The first time,

she took my hands
    and showed me
        the dark, fluttery grass

between her legs.
    The fuzzy orange perfume
        of her vagina

burned straight up
    in my nostrils.
        Two, perhaps three, times

I thought I had an erection
    and she opened her legs
        and I leaned forward

and my penis began to soften,
      go away.
            She always took out

two glasses of water
      but I never raised one
            to my lips.

Once she stopped me
      in the middle of the afternoon
            and offered to remove

my clothes.
      When she pulled off
            my underwear

I was almost her son,
      my eyes looking back
            with the barest of color.

What Kind of Dark It Is

When she wants
        to make love
                I find myself

in a room
        with someone
                I don't know.

So
        I tell her
                about my life

again.
        I take her body
                between

my arms.
        And then
                I change

the position
        of my head
                on the pillow,

moment
        to moment,
                remembering

the precise
        architecture
                of the windows,

but forgetting
        the face
                I am looking into.

Night, Now

At the end
of the evening,
when you would come

into the bedroom
wearing a large blousy
white T-shirt,

filling the room
with a lilac-scented soap,
and sit on the edge

of the bed
and slide your legs
beneath the blanket,

trying not to touch me,
you always did.
You said

it wasn't so bad,
and rubbed my chest,
the circles of hair

that rise from the belly.
Did you know
when you pressed your mouth

against my mouth
just before you turned
your body toward the wall,

the city lay down?
    There was a star
        deep in the floor.

In the windows,
    blank photographs.
        Sometimes late at night

I'd wake and wonder
    whose problem am I,
        whose son?

Father and Son

I was joking
        (there was always
                that)

when I moved
        my fingers down
                the buttons

of her blouse
        and then around
                the knots

of the breasts.
        When she moved
                her legs apart,

I took her thighs
        in my hands
                and rubbed

them down
        and up.
                And then

I stood
        and walked
                into the bathroom

to see
        how I looked
                in the mirror

when the dark rises
        above the neck.
                Eyes

I could live with
        without seeing.
                Then,

the water.
        Fuck you, I said,
                and stood still.

Invisible Bride

Is your face the wind that blows so hard
I have to shout? Well,

I won't go to work today or, worse, cover my ears.

A woman with a long dress is today out
of her house and pointing up the road.

You know what now is being done?

I can hear her calling,
the snow falling into the cold water of a pool.

Jason, get up. I thought it was you.

You

Stand close,
    inhale my breath.
        You're my shadow,

even in the dark.
    We were born to love,
        sooner or later.

We're humans.
    Aren't we?
        Don't leave

until you slip
    into the sleeves
        of my shirt.

Say something—
    and it's about
        something else

but not about us—
    which is a kind
        of loving.

For a long time
    the long falling
        of light

in the trees.
    Nothing changes.
        And the people

you've known,
        let's invite them all
            to dinner.

Of No Change, and Worse, Change

Irene asks
       for money.
              I come up

with some.
       She waits,
              hands in pockets.

You sure?
       When the movie
              is over

I follow
       a different woman
              down

a rainy street.
       *I will always
              love you*, I say.

Later,
       I look outside
              the window

to see what kind
       of cars
              people drive.

Knees drawn
       to my chin
              it breaks my heart

when the late night
        TV show is over.
                Irene brings her tarot cards

to the kitchen table,
        her belly hanging out
                above her panties.

A Version of the Future

Irene is sick
    of having to work
        as a proofreader,

the words
    on the page
        no words at all,

but a sticky,
    bluish-black
        substance of acid

and alcohol.
    And the Green Line
        of the subway

broken again.
    I can hear her sighs
        coming out

of my mouth
    in a dark room
        at the end of a hall,

music
    from a radio
        set to play

the same song
    every morning
        at eight o'clock.

Maybe
    I should invite her
        to sit

at my famous friend's
    dinner table.
        Maybe

help find work
    for the woman inside
        of her who never

lets her sleep.
    Who's to say
        where it all began?

Brooklyn for me?
    San Francisco for her?
        It was something

different
    for each of us.
        Yet it was the same.

I had a father
    but he died.
        She had a father

but he died.
    I have this dream, she says,
        blouse open,

drink in her hand.
   It's possible,
    No?

No.
   But every time
    I say *Yes.*

Woman Undressing

Sometimes I will stand up and leave.

And, another time, I will remain but only stay
so long. There's a moment I am mad with grief,

seeing no one. Close my eyes and glimpse
a glint of light lying down in a field.

The Furniture of My Own Neglect

The sheets
    you gave me
        should have been changed

by now
    but they are just
        the same, too—

like the towels
    I keep washing
        my face with

a long time
    after they're rotted.
        Except when you enter,

love,
    and then, also—
        a city made dark

by throwing
    a shirt over a lamp.
        I turn a string

through the holes
    in my sneakers,
        broken before I was born.

Except When You Enter

I notice my old love
    walking with someone
        and I gesture

with my glasses
    should she recognize me.
        I write this line

and fix her safely
    within it,
        and hope my poems

appear in magazines
    she reads.
        As she stands

in the kitchen
    stirring her husband's soup,
        I hope her eyes fall

on my name
    and the terrible
        mistake of her life

becomes clear.
    I will then pray
        for a small earthquake.

The cries of the fallen
    reach me
        and I free everyone

except her.
      Years later
           I find her

asleep
      and carry her back
           to my room

where she remembers
      nothing
           but how I saved her.

The Past

All the waves want to come in at once.

Stars rush toward earth.

Every desire has a degree in which angels
lend an ear.

After all, I'm not in the world yet.

The presence of someone has come upon me.
What is the past if I can change?

The Presence of Someone

Where
> *have you been?*
>> she whispered.

Nowhere.
> *I haven't been*
>> *anywhere.*

I'm not even here, I said.
> In front
>> of a window,

opening a car door
> in a parking lot,
>> placing a plate

on the table,
> some words slipped
>> out of her mouth.

And then her
> lopsided head,
>> stony face,

turned toward mine,
> giving up
>> the top half

of her lips,
> whose bottom half
>> was jelly.

This is the kiss
        between us, she said.
                And once,

the fragrance
        of many flowers
                and my tongue,

the heavy trapdoor
        of a vault
                the wind suddenly lifted.

Good Night Irene

It's the last hour,
    the very last hour.
        And all the windows

are closed.
    When I mention
        the word love,

keeping it on my tongue,
    you say, Yes—
        What time is it, Irene?

Are you ready?
    You wore nothing
        under a black silk robe,

a glass of wine
    on the table.
        You swore never to hurry.

Where is your mouth, Irene,
    dressed in purple
        with a promise

of Spring?
    Is it time, Irene?
        Another working day?

Whichever way I move myself
    I can't enter
        the kitchen, Irene.

Maybe
      there is no such thing
         as us —

for the spirit flowers
      without stop
         without ever knowing

it is us,
      so when you leave
         we are not lessened, Irene.

Maybe I just want
      to be adored.
         Maybe it's cold

inside the body
      no matter how close you are.
         Maybe

I'll be the woman
      I need.
         Ocean. Irene.

We are ocean.
      Night. Irene.
         We are night.

Stars.
      A thousand times stars
         and a thousand times stars

tearing themselves apart, Irene,
    long ago,
        the last of their light

glittering
    in the sky
        when they are laid out just so, Irene.

The Beginning of Love

I go to my love
    the way I go to the ocean.
        I lie down

for her like a raft
    when the wish to float
        no longer matters.

I am the angel
    the cold leaves
        in her breath.

I open up her heart
    like a rose
        and pull the bee out.

Sometimes, late at night,
    I sit on the edge
        of the bed imagining

the shape of words
    that will comfort her.
        In August I wrap

a cold towel
    around her forehead.
        I always take out

two glasses. When I open
    the car door for her
        I can't imagine anything

but staying at home,
     lying in bed,
          staying at home.

And when she's away
     I can see her through
          the moon falling

on the floor
     in the shape
          of an hourglass.

Morning

There are stones on the beach
I should have guessed

were birds blown away from the rest.

They are speckled with white and gray and green
as if a painter overpainted.

If you ask me anything about it,

I will go on telling you the same thing—
to be in love is like going outside

to see what kind of day it is.

What Kind of Day It Is

Birds turning their wings
    but look again
        they are gone

into another sky
    but not for long
        the air let out

of the moon
    whizzing and sinking
        in the window

the tiger coming back
    even before
        it ever was a tiger

and glowing
    whenever it is touched
        a star spinning

clouds melting
    in the ceiling
        into great drops

of sunlight
    drifts of dust
        pockets of powder

the golden apples
    in a bowl
        after they are gone

someone watching
    from the fringes
        someone waiting

for something to happen
    set the big blue boat
        on the water

Forty Years Gone One Night

It wasn't so bad
     being on the wrong side
          of my father's belt buckle

because when it was over
     for good
          there was each truly

astonished hair rising.
     Or my mother
          could be touching me

and she could say
     it was to awaken.
          But I know

I can be handsome
     if I want.
          Once I tried

to make myself married,
     but I wasn't used to standing
          on the tips

of my toes. I should have
     made love more
          and made it dark for a purpose.

Man on Bed

When Irene lay
    under the sheets,
        late morning,

and turned her back,
    I sat on the edge
        of the bed,

sunlight passing
    through my fingers
        and throwing itself

on the floor
    lying there—
        a vision

I could put
    my hands on.
        Who's to say

I couldn't be stripped
    of everything
        but what I feared—

a brightness
    and hold it up
        against my lips

and then I'd know
    what it was
        and wake her?

Invisible Groom

To feel the intimacy
    of my friends
        is a good thing

as in a room
    a small bulb burning
        a little light

— but the tenderness
    that comes from those
        I don't know

has become a fire
    that burns
        even after the fire

is out.
    To anyone
        walking hurriedly by

without stopping
    without ever knowing
        I was there—

their not-touching
    has become the one thing
        I lie down with.

Man Undressing

The dye in the hair will go on for a while.
The shirt in the mirror is in style.

I have done. I have done.

Tell me when it's all right. How it is with me.
And then I'll remember too.

And I'll lean my shoulder into your shoulder
into whatever comes.

Because One Is Always Leaving

Especially
        in the late afternoon,
                when my nieces

close their eyes
        and bend
                their heads

to inhale
        the bubbles that rise
                from the tall glasses

of milk,
        licking the juice
                off their lips

that open
        on the softened
                black-and-white cookies

that have been
        dipped
                into the glass

and then dipped
        again,
                sopping with cream,

I like to think
        about stopping
                the passage of time—

not a bird,
      not a branch
           in bloom,

not an insect
      stirring
           in the still grasses and ferns.

Especially in the Late Afternoon

The warm air makes us
    different
        from the way

we are.
    We go deep
        in the long grasses and ferns

at the edge
    of an open field.
        Is it knowing

what to do
    with the long-stemmed lilac
        that counts?

It's dark.
    Or it will be.
        Some trees perfectly still,

which only this morning
    thrashed about
        in a storm.

Your hand
    has found mine.
        Have we ever arrived

in the arms of someone
    who wasn't lost
        from the start?

The Water That Moves the River Along

In the middle of my life
    a little girl
        runs toward me.

Maybe she thinks
    I'm her father.
        It's the gray whiskers

and the hat.
    She takes my right leg
        between her arms,

and then pulls
    on my sleeve,
        wanting something

I don't have,
    and cries—
        tears she never imagined

and whatever she does
    to stop them
        does not.

Is it
    that even her father
        will not have something

for her?
    What is it?
    What?

And then
        another little girl
                rushes forward

and cries
        over the cries
                of the other,

the curious gathering
        in a circle
                I'm in the middle of.

Another Man

I am afraid to look
    at the beauty
        in a man's face,

whiskers collecting
    on his cheeks,
        scruffy with romance.

I was thinking
    of something different,
        I guess—

as if the body
    were single-jointed.
        What is it that the heart

does not want
    to attend to?
        I can almost remember

when I was a girl,
    hairless. As if
        I could lean out

of a window, dreaming
    of another man,
        sometimes I have wanted

to bow my head
    and kiss my sad,
        skinny belly.

For Later

As it turns out,
    I don't know
        if I'll remember

the precise architecture
    of Irene's face,
        hair falling

across her forehead.
    What was it
        that moved

through her eyes
    the color of the moon
        and was gone?

Rain collecting
    on her cheeks—
        a faint perfume

of lilacs
    after they are gone.
        Love, be the voice

that calls to me
    but has nothing to say.
        Let me lean out

of a window
    thinking of the beauty
        of your face

not to keep
      but to hold
            long enough to change.

The Future

Right now, somewhere, you are forgetting me.
My God, I'm vanishing!

Am I dead?

Not quite—but undesired.
What was it I was that should be remembered?

Especially in the Evening

Night falls
  and on its way
    it takes its time

in the open air
  not yet really dark
    —light, even.

Still growing-time.
  But I know
    that's not how it is,

not only—
  What will become
  of us,

not yet really loved,
  betrayed, even?
    Defenseless waiting—

too much, always,
  then, too little.
    Is it the dark

that we can't see
  as long
    as we're in it?

One Day I Will Die

How proud I am
        to be the center
                of a tragedy.

Again
        and again
                the same shadow.

Thank you God.
        Thank you shadow.
                Happy is the man

who looks into
        the deepest folds
                of his sorrows.

The soul, lost,
        can be stirred.
                Thank you sorrows.

Thank you
        bottom of the river.
                Won't you be forever?

No one else
        in sight.
                Soon I won't

have to work
        to get attention.
                Thank you work.

Haven't you carried me
        everywhere?
                And thank you

silence
        for holding me
                before I spoke.

And it does no good
        to give me a glass
                of water.

And it does no good
        to wipe the sweat
                from my forehead.

Not now.
        Not in the night
                with my eyes closing.

Thank you night.
        This time
                before I leave

I want to thank
        my friends.
                Thank you friends.

Thank you.
        What more could I,
                a dying man, want?

Man Dying

I had no idea that in the middle of my life
I would become used to my own absence.

Something can be done, always? I ask,
folding every shirt.

And I say, How else can I live?
And I say, This, this way.

Man Dressing

When I am dressing
      I sit a long time
            looking at my shirts.

I do not know
      which one will be
            the one I choose,

but I see each one
      has taken a style
            of its own—smooth,

rough, or radiant.
      I love the open-collar
            soft denim.

Its wavy sky blue
      brightens the blue
            in my eyes

my sister says.
      I've never seen
            a color like it

except lying down once
      on a sloping field
            in West Copake, New York,

and looking up.
      When did I get
            so many—

and yet choose only one
        every day?
                Before

slipping my arms
        sideways
                into their sleeves,

I unbutton
        the buttons
                and press

every pore of my face
        in their chests
                and sometimes

underneath
        their armpits.
                When I have

stepped inside
        of the one I choose
                I stand

before the tall mirror.
        I love to see
                if I have changed,

if I'm less worried.
        I'm so lucky
                I have found

the one.
>It is the only one
>>I could have found.

I am
>the only one
>>who could have found it.

The End of Love

When I go to sleep,
    I'm afraid
        to take off

my shirt
    and have nothing
        to lie next to.

I love to press
    my face
        into every pore

of a pillow,
    feathers
        stopping my mouth,

and then
    turn my face
        suddenly

staring
    at my reflection
        in the wall.

That was great, I say.
    And great
        the moonlight

curving off
    the edge
        of my toes.

And great
  the angels slipping
    through an opening

in the sky.
  Only the body lying
    outside the heart

is safe.
  You understand?
    Anyway,

the crevice
  below my nose
    is where my mother pressed

her forefinger
  to open my lips.
    When I have the last

sensation of the day,
  I move my hands
    to that place.

How else can I live?
  Sleep of the secrets
    my body has kept

from me.
  Sleep of the women
    I've never gotten

close to,
      inhaling their breath.
            Death lasts a year

at most
      but love is forever!
            Sure, I'm mistaken.

Sure, I'm the wind.
      But what's even more
            terrific?

I'm also the sky,
      and the pocket
            I put my hand into,

and the last light out,
      saying, everything
            that has come before

and everything
      that will come after
            will be new.

If ever
      I had something to say
            it should be now,

but I forget.
      You understand?
            Someone may want

to kiss me
        but only my soul
                wants to kiss me

enough, asleep
        in my arms
                as I fall

asleep.
        It is trying
                to tell me something.

Acknowledgments

Thanks to the editors of the following magazines in which some of the poems in this collection, sometimes in different versions, first appeared: *Agni, American Poetry Review, Good Foot,* the *Kenyon Review, Michigan Quarterly Review, Nerve, PIF, Provincetown Arts,* and *Tin House.* Thanks also to the editors of the following anthologies in which poems in this collection also appeared: *Outsiders: Poems of Exile* and *Roots and Flowers.*

The poem "Except When You Enter" (as "Work") and a line or lines in select poems including "Getting Laid," "A Version of the Future," "Good Night Irene," and "The End of Love" are reprinted from *Every Room We Ever Slept In* © Jason Shinder. The poem "My Father's House" was inspired by the poem "Having It Out with Melancholy" by Jane Kenyon, and the poem "Man Dying" was inspired by the poem "The Gate" by Marie Howe.

For every faith and freedom, Sophie Cabot Black.

My thanks to the following people who provided *invaluable support* and comments regarding the poems in this collection, without whom the book would not have been possible: Katie Adams, Steven Bauer, Laurel Blossom, Tony Hoagland, Marie Howe, Stanley Kunitz, Sheila Murphy, and Liz Rosenberg.

My thanks also to Fiona McCrae, Jeffrey Shotts, and Fred Marchant from Graywolf Press. And thanks to April Bernard, Alice Mattison, and Askold Melnyczuk for their understanding and support, as well as to my colleagues and students at Bennington College, and to the folks at *George's Pizzeria* and *Stormy Harbour.*

"Because One Is Always Leaving" is for Jamie and Jennah Kudler. "What Kind of Day It Is" is for Fiona Cabot Scanlon-Black.

About the Author

JASON SHINDER's first book of poems, *Every Room We Ever Slept In*, was a New York Public Library Notable Book, and he has received awards or fellowships from the Fine Arts Work Center in Provincetown, Massachusetts, the California State Arts Council, the National Endowment for the Arts, and the Yaddo Corporation, among others. He is the editor of several anthologies including, most recently, *Tales from the Couch: Writers on Therapy* and *First Books* and is Series Editor of the annual series *Best American Movie Writing*. A book of his interviews with poets on poets of the past, *What Thou Lovest Well Remains*, is forthcoming. He is on the faculty of the graduate writing programs at Bennington College and New School University, and was recently Poet-in-Residence at the State University of New York at Binghamton. Founder and director of the YMCA National Writer's Voice and YMCA of the USA Arts and Humanities, he is also the director of Sundance Institute's Writing Program.

The text of *Among Women* is set in Berling, a typeface designed by the Swedish typographer and calligrapher Karl-Erik Forsberg, and issued in 1951 by the Berlingska Stilgjuteriet Foundry in Lund, Sweden. Book design by Wendy Holdman. Set in type by Stanton Publication Services, Inc., and manufactured by Bang Printing on acid-free paper.

Graywolf Press is a not-for-profit, independent press. The books we publish include poetry, literary fiction, essays, and cultural criticism. We are less interested in best-sellers than in talented writers who display a freshness of voice coupled with a distinct vision. We believe these are the very qualities essential to shape a vital and diverse culture.

Thankfully, many of our readers feel the same way. They have shown this through their desire to buy books by Graywolf writers; they have told us this themselves through their e-mail notes and at author events; and they have reinforced their commitment by contributing financial support, in small amounts and in large amounts, and joining the "Friends of Graywolf."

If you enjoyed this book and wish to learn more about Graywolf Press, we invite you to ask your bookseller or librarian about further Graywolf titles; or to contact us for a free catalog; or to visit our award-winning web site that features information about our forthcoming books.

We would also like to invite you to consider joining the hundreds of individuals who are already "Friends of Graywolf" by contributing to our membership program. Individual donations of any size are significant to us: they tell us that you believe that the kind of publishing we do *matters*. Our web site gives you many more details about the benefits you will enjoy as a "Friend of Graywolf"; but if you do not have online access, we urge you to contact us for a copy of our membership brochure.

www.graywolfpress.org

Graywolf Press
2402 University Avenue, Suite 203
Saint Paul, MN 55114
Phone: (651) 641-0077
Fax: (651) 641-0036
E-mail: wolves@graywolfpress.org

Graywolf Press is dedicated to the creation and promotion of thoughtful and imaginative contemporary literature essential to a vital and diverse culture. For further information, visit us online at: **www.graywolfpress.org**.

Other Graywolf titles you might enjoy are:

Bewitched Playground by David Rivard
Donkey Gospel by Tony Hoagland
Full Moon Boat by Fred Marchant
Otherwise: New & Selected Poems by Jane Kenyon
Pastoral by Carl Phillips
Some Ether by Nick Flynn
The Way It Is by William Stafford
Things and Flesh by Linda Gregg